How Whales Walked Into the Sea

by
FAITH McNULTY

illustrated by
TED RAND

Scholastic Press
NEW YORK

ISBN 0-590-89830-2

Text copyright © 1999 by Faith McNulty • Illustrations copyright © 1999 by Ted Rand
All rights reserved. Published by Scholastic Press, a division of Scholastic Inc.,
Publishers since 1920. scholastic and scholastic press and associated logos are trademarks
and/or registered trademarks of Scholastic Inc.

Library of Congress Cataloging-in-Publication Number: 98-061211

10 9 8 7 6 5 4 3 2 1   9/9 0/0 01 02 03 04 • First edition, February 1999 • Printed in Mexico   49

The text type was set in copperplate 32bc and copperplate 33bc • The display type was set in Caflisch
Script MM Swash 556 Semibold • For the illustrations, Ted Rand used acrylic paints, watercolor paints, and
chalk on rag stock • Book design by Marijka Kostiw

To Charlie, John, and Richard
—F.M.

To my new grandson, Roy Willis
—T.R.

WHALES ARE STRANGE ANIMALS. THEY ARE AMONG THE STRANGEST ON EARTH. THEY LIVE IN THE SEA, BUT THEY ARE NOT FISH. THE BODIES OF FISH ARE AS COLD AS THE SEA THEY SWIM IN. THE BODIES OF WHALES ARE WARM, EVEN WHEN THEY SWIM IN ICY WATER. FISH ARE BORN FROM EGGS. A WHALE IS BORN FROM ITS MOTHER'S BODY.

Humpback Whale

Mesonychid

LONG AGO, PEOPLE BELIEVED THAT WHALES WERE HALF FISH, HALF LAND ANIMAL. NOW WE KNOW THAT THE ANCESTORS OF WHALES WERE FURRY, FOUR-LEGGED ANIMALS THAT LIVED ON LAND. FOSSIL BONES TELL THE STORY. IT BEGINS FIFTY MILLION YEARS AGO. THE WORLD WAS DIFFERENT THEN. THE OCEANS WERE WIDER AND NOT AS DEEP AS THEY ARE TODAY. THE WEATHER WAS WARMER. PLANTS AND ANIMALS FOUND PLENTY OF FOOD AT THE EDGES OF THE WARM, SHALLOW SEAS.

TODAY, MILLIONS OF YEARS LATER, WE FIND THE OUTLINES OF THEIR BODIES PRESSED INTO STONE AND ARE ABLE TO GUESS WHAT THEY LOOKED LIKE. AS THE YEARS PASSED, MANY SPECIES BECAME EXTINCT. OTHERS WERE ABLE TO CHANGE AS THE WORLD CHANGED. THEY BECAME THE ANCESTORS OF THE ANIMALS WE KNOW TODAY.

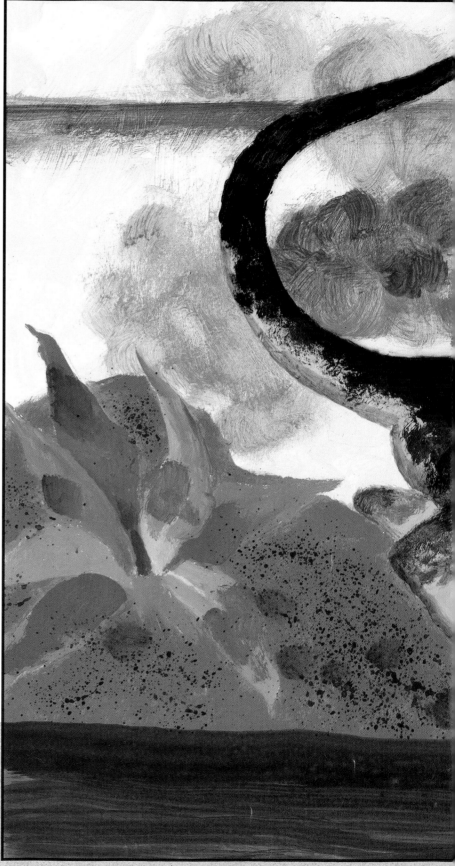

Among the animals that lived then was a group called mesonychids. They had four legs, fur, sharp teeth, and long tails. They nursed their young with milk. Some were as small as cats. Some were as big as bears. And some were in-between. These animals, the mesonychids, ate meat — any kind they could find. They liked fish, too.

Mesonychid

MESONYCHIDS THAT LIVED NEAR RIVERS OR AT THE EDGE OF THE SEA WADED INTO THE WATER TO CATCH FISH. THEY FOUND IT EASIER TO CATCH FISH THAN TO HUNT ON LAND. AND SAFER, TOO. THE BIG, DANGEROUS ANIMALS THAT LIKED TO HUNT MESONYCHIDS COULD NOT SWIM. WE CAN PICTURE A MESONYCHID WADING IN SHALLOW WATER, THEN GOING DEEPER TO CHASE ITS PREY.

Mesonychid

Mesonychid

LITTLE BY LITTLE, IT LEARNS TO SWIM. NOW IT CAN GO FAR FROM SHORE AND HUNT BIGGER FISH. SOME MESONYCHIDS WERE BETTER SWIMMERS THAN OTHERS. THOSE WITH BROAD FEET LIKE PADDLES SWAM FASTER AND CAUGHT MORE FISH. THEIR CHILDREN AND GRAND-CHILDREN HAD BROAD FEET, TOO. AFTER THOUSANDS OF YEARS AND THOUSANDS OF GENERATIONS, ALL THE MESONYCHIDS THAT SWAM FAR FROM SHORE HAD BROAD FEET. THIS IS JUST ONE OF THE CHANGES THAT HAPPENED, LITTLE BY LITTLE, AS THE MESONYCHIDS BECAME MORE SUITED TO LIFE IN THE SEA.

After a few million years, the swimming mesonychids were quite different from their cousins on land. Fossil bones show how they had changed. They had become the animal we call *Ambulocetus* — the Walking Whale. It was about ten feet long. It had a long jaw and sharp teeth for catching prey. Its short, broad legs were good for swimming. It was at home in the water, but went onto the land to rest and give birth to its young.

Ambulocetus

Rodhocetus

BUT CHANGE IN ANIMALS NEVER STOPS. THE WALKING WHALE WENT ON CHANGING. WE HAVE NOT FOUND THE BONES THAT SHOW EACH STEP, BUT WE HAVE THE BONES OF AN ANIMAL FARTHER ALONG THE ROAD TO BECOMING A WHALE. IT IS CALLED *RODHOCETUS* — THE HARDLY WALKING WHALE. THE HIND LEGS OF THE HARDLY WALKING WHALE WERE SO SMALL, THEY COULD BARELY CARRY ITS BODY. IT SPENT MOST OF ITS LIFE IN THE SEA AND CAME TO SHORE ONLY TO GIVE BIRTH. ON LAND, IT WAS EASY PREY FOR BIGGER ANIMALS, BUT IN THE WATER IT WAS STRONG AND AGILE. ITS BODY WAS LONG AND TAPERED, ALMOST LIKE THE BODIES OF WHALES TODAY. ITS TAIL WAS BROAD AT THE END.

THE HARDLY WALKING WHALE USED ITS TAIL LIKE A PADDLE TO DRIVE ITS BODY THROUGH THE WATER. THIS IS THE WAY WHALES SWIM TODAY.

Still, changes went on and on. In another few million years, the Hardly Walking Whale had disappeared. New forms took its place. Each new form was more and more like the whales that live in the ocean today. One of them was an animal we call *Dorudon*. It was almost like a modern whale, but it still had small hind legs. Since it never came on land, its legs were useless and would later disappear.

Dorudon

Bowhead Whale

MODERN WHALES — OUR WHALES — FIRST APPEARED THIRTY MILLION YEARS AGO. THEY ARE PERFECTLY FITTED TO LIFE IN THE SEA. THEY ARE LARGE. A THICK LAYER OF FAT CALLED BLUBBER KEEPS THEM WARM IN CHILLY SEAWATER. WHERE EARS USED TO BE, THERE ARE ONLY TINY HOLES. A WHALE DOESN'T NEED OUTER EARS. IT CAN HEAR UNDERWATER THROUGH THE BONES OF ITS SKULL AND JAW. THE FUR OF ITS ANCESTORS IS GONE, TOO, EXCEPT FOR A FEW WHISKERS ON ITS UPPER LIP OR CHIN. A WHALE HAS NO HIND LEGS, BUT TINY LEG BONES ARE HIDDEN INSIDE ITS BODY — THE ONLY REMAINS OF THE LEGS ITS ANCESTORS HAD. FORELEGS ARE NOW FLIPPERS — BROAD PADDLES THAT STICK OUT LIKE WINGS. INSIDE THE FLIPPERS ARE ARM, WRIST, AND FINGER BONES. THEY ARE JUST LIKE THOSE OF THE LAND ANIMALS THAT WENT INTO THE WATER SO MANY MILLIONS OF YEARS AGO.

One of the strangest changes is the way in which a whale breathes. Its nostrils are on the top of its head. A whale can take a breath of air without raising its head out of the water. A whale can hold its breath for a long time — ten or fifteen minutes — while it dives deep in search of food. When it comes to the surface, it blows stale air out of its blowhole in a misty spout.

Killer Whale

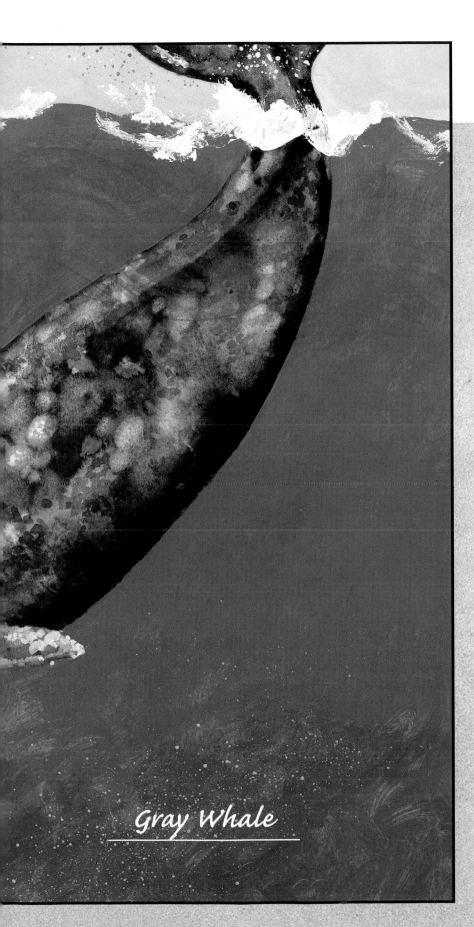

Gray Whale

WHALES ARE DIVIDED INTO TWO GROUPS — WHALES WITH TEETH AND WHALES THAT HAVE BALEEN IN PLACE OF TEETH. BALEEN GROWS FROM THE ROOF OF THE WHALE'S MOUTH IN BONY STRIPS THAT FORM A FINE-TOOTHED COMB. IT IS USED TO CATCH THE SMALL FISH AND TINY SEA CREATURES CALLED KRILL THAT ARE THE BALEEN WHALE'S ONLY FOOD. BALEEN WHALES FEED BY TAKING IN A MOUTHFUL OF WATER AND SQUIRTING IT OUT THROUGH THE BALEEN, THEN SWALLOWING WHATEVER IS LEFT BEHIND.

Sperm Whale

THE SPERM WHALE IS A HUGE
TOOTHED WHALE. IT EATS SQUID
AND OCTOPUS, BONELESS ANIMALS
THAT HAVE TENTACLES. WE CAN
IMAGINE SPERM WHALES AND
GIANT OCTOPUSES FIGHTING
MIGHTY BATTLES IN THE DEPTHS
OF THE SEA.

Blue Whale

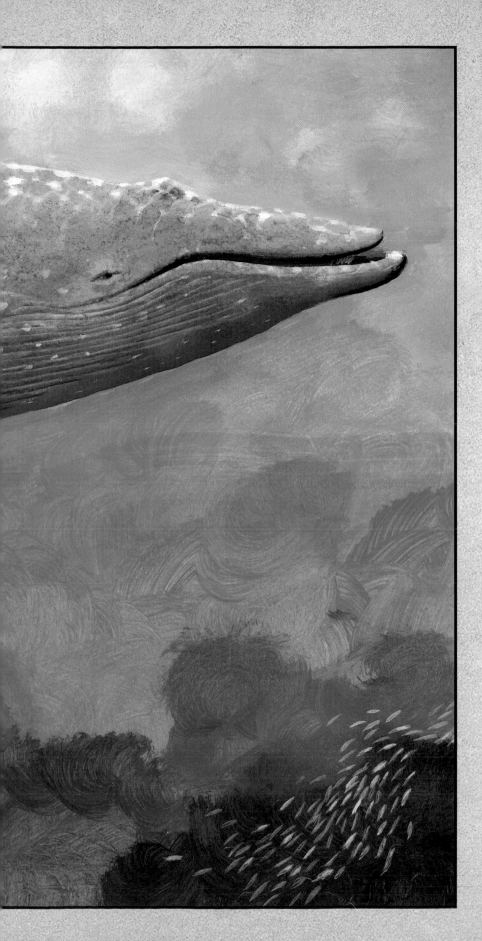

BABY WHALES ARE BORN UNDER-
WATER. THE NEWBORN QUICKLY
SWIMS UP FOR A BREATH OF AIR.
ITS MOTHER NURSES IT WITH MILK,
AND PROTECTS IT JUST AS LAND
ANIMALS PROTECT THEIR YOUNG.
SOME YOUNG WHALES SWIM BY
THEIR MOTHERS' SIDES FOR TWO
YEARS OR MORE.

LIKE MANY LAND ANIMALS,
WHALES LIVE IN FAMILY GROUPS:
FEMALES AND YOUNG CLOSEST
TOGETHER; MALES AT A DISTANCE,
BUT STILL PART OF THE HERD.
UNDER WATER, WHERE THE LIGHT
IS TOO DIM AND THEY CANNOT SEE
EACH OTHER, THEY PROBABLY KEEP
IN TOUCH WITH SOUNDS.

We know that whales make sounds, strange to our ears, that remind us of music. Listening to whales, we hear what we call "songs," but have no way of knowing what they mean.

We know a great deal about the bodies of whales, but very little about their minds. They have very large brains. We know they think and have feelings. But we can only try to imagine what it is like to live a life eternally in the sea.

What is it like to roam forever with no one place that is home? What is it like to dive into deep, cold water — dark as a cave — and then come up into light and air? Does the whale still have some of the feelings of a land animal, just as it has finger bones hidden in its flippers? Does the whale still love the sun?

THE WHALES

THE **HUMPBACK** IS A LARGE BALEEN WHALE. IT IS BLACK WITH WHITE PATCHES AND HAS LONG, WINGLIKE FLIPPERS. THE HUMPBACK IS THE MOST PLAYFUL WHALE. IT OFTEN LEAPS OUT OF THE WATER AND STANDS ON ITS TAIL, AS THOUGH TO LOOK AROUND, BEFORE IT FALLS WITH A HUGE SPLASH.

THE **BOWHEAD WHALE** HAS A SLIM BODY AND A HUGE HEAD AND MOUTH. IT LIVES IN ICY ARCTIC WATERS THAT CONTAIN GREAT SWARMS OF THE TINY PLANTS AND ANIMALS ON WHICH THE BOWHEAD FEEDS. A BOWHEAD WHALE CAN EAT MORE THAN A TON OF THIS FOOD A DAY. UNFORTUNATELY, SO MANY BOWHEADS HAVE BEEN KILLED BY WHALERS THAT THERE ARE NOW VERY FEW LEFT.

THE **ORCA**, ALSO KNOWN AS THE **KILLER WHALE**, IS RELATED TO DOLPHINS AND OTHER SMALL WHALES WITH TEETH. IN THE WILD, KILLER WHALES ROAM THE OCEAN IN PACKS, HUNTING FISH, BIRDS, SEALS, AND EVEN BALEEN WHALES. IN CAPTIVITY, WHERE THEY ARE WELL FED, THEY ARE GENTLE AND FRIENDLY TO PEOPLE.

THE HEAD OF A **SPERM WHALE** IS SHAPED LIKE A BOX. ON TOP OF ITS SKULL IS A CAVITY FILLED WITH AN OILY LIQUID CALLED SPERMACETI. NO ONE KNOWS WHAT WHALES USE IT FOR. THE SPERM WHALE'S NARROW MOUTH IS ON THE UNDERSIDE OF THIS CASE.

THE **BLUE WHALE** IS THE LARGEST BALEEN WHALE. IT CAN GROW AS LONG AS A HUNDRED FEET AND AS HIGH AS A TWO-STORY HOUSE. ITS BLOOD FLOWS THROUGH ARTERIES AS BIG AROUND AS STOVE PIPES; ITS HEART WEIGHS A THOUSAND POUNDS. THE BLUE WHALE IS BIGGER THAN ANY DINOSAUR AND MAY BE THE LARGEST ANIMAL THAT HAS EVER LIVED.

GRAY WHALES ARE BALEEN WHALES ABOUT FIFTY FEET LONG THAT LIVE IN THE PACIFIC OCEAN. THEY SPEND THE SUMMERS IN THE FAR NORTH AND TRAVEL SOUTH TO GIVE BIRTH TO THEIR YOUNG IN WARMER WATERS. DURING THESE JOURNEYS, THEY SWIM SO CLOSE TO THE CALIFORNIA COAST THAT THEY CAN BE SEEN FROM A SMALL BOAT, OR EVEN FROM THE SHORE.

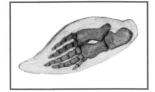

INSIDE WHALES' FLIPPERS ARE ARM, WRIST, AND FINGER BONES. THEY ARE JUST LIKE THOSE OF THE LAND ANIMALS THAT WENT INTO THE WATER SO MANY MILLIONS OF YEARS AGO.